Dear Mr. Brancusi

poems by

Melora Walters

Finishing Line Press
Georgetown, Kentucky

Dear Mr. Brancusi

This book is dedicated to John and Pauline Borking

ACKNOWLEDGMENTS

Special thanks to Leah Maines, Chiwan Choi, and Alan Wertheimer.

Guest Editor: Leah Maines

Editor: Christen Kincaid

Cover Art: Melora Walters

Author Photo: Mira Sorvino

Cover Design: Elizabeth Maines

Printed in the USA on acid-free paper.
Order online: www.finishinglinepress.com
              also available on amazon.com

Author inquiries and mail orders:
Finishing Line Press
P. O. Box 1626
Georgetown, Kentucky 40324
U. S. A.

Table of Contents

Later That Night

The letter continued:

today I visited your atelier,
next to the Pompidou.
I was jet lagged and disillusioned,
out of breath, out of luck, empty of —

The writer stopped,
looked around the room, the window
slightly opened earlier for fresh air.
Snowflakes were coming in.
It was dark.

After turning off the light,
the eyes become accustomed;
objects are ghosts that emerge
and reach out to call to dead gods
that are not dead because they cannot—

in paralysis in the shape of an airplane seat,
in paralysis in the shape of blackened memories,
in the paralysis of a Pompeian volcanic ash figure—

she went back to the letter:

I was jet lagged and disillusioned.
I no longer cared for Paris,
this place I had been dreaming of.
I felt trapped;
the hotel room felt cobwebbed
with past exchanges,
soft from the silk threads—
a hammock of dirt to hold
and sway in a tremor.

She began again:

Stepping inside your atelier,

I felt hope.
Did you know that it is still free?
The arrangement of the tools
by your hands made me

She stopped.

Your search for pure form.

She stopped again.

I am sorry you died alone.

Mr. Brancusi,

I would give up everything
to lie with you in the loft area,
to lie there and watch you work.
I love your hands.
I would give up everything
to bring you coffee and cook for you.

As she wrote, she knew she wouldn't,
and it would show itself in the dried
coffee grinds in the overturned cups,
that she would read to him as he drew,
secretly looking for her own answers.

Let me start over.

Dear Mr. Brancusi,

Where I live, mist comes down over the mountains.
It is a Chinese painting not made in China.
Clouds rest on the streets, the tops of trees,
draping themselves anywhere
like a woman collapsed,
one arm above her head.

Let me start again:

The sky is pregnant.
Birds sing at different hours of the day.
A lizard climbs.

Your photograph hangs on my wall.

In the Water

Long dark hairs intertwine around my fingers.
I watch them.
They could be thin veins in an invisible hand trying to hold mine
or they could be sent to pull me down into the depths.
They could be anything.
I am just lying here in the water
that is getting cold.

There is only the trying to not drown.

      * * *

I woke up and realized that I had been camping
in my house like a gypsy.

I did not know how to start living in it
until I measured the perimeter of the property
for the brush clearance of this
Very High Fire Hazard Severity Zone.

I climbed the hill and stood with the map in one hand
and the measuring tape in the other.

This is it,
I thought,
this is where I live.

      * * *

A man's shadow emerges from the top of the shadow of the
building behind me. The shadow man picks up a ladder and

climbs beyond the building in front of me, the one that holds the
shadow on its gray cinder blocked wall. He disappears.
I watch the shadow man climb the shadow ladder into the sky
and vanish.

Imagine that I did not know that it was a shadow,
that I thought it was real.
I watched a man climb the wall into the sky
and disappear right in front of my eyes.
I ask myself what that means, *right in front of my eyes.*
It was there. I swore I could touch it.

Imagine, though, that I believed it was real, that I felt
I had a visitation, that I change my whole life around this.

But we, you, the reader, and I, know that it was nothing
but a shadow of something mundane—
a man was fixing something on the roof.

            *   *   *

Old photographs are dangerous.

Land mines.

            *   *   *

The gardener stepped on a rattlesnake near the corner of our
fence. He told me it was accidental. He had to kill it.

It was easy to kill, he said. No need to worry. He left it there
because he knew that the other one would show up as they do,
or as they did in Arkansas on my grandparent's farm.
But the other one never appeared.

It's there now lying in the dirt. Invisible, until you see it
and your breath comes out at a different angle.
And then there is nothing but it, the landscape,
radiating from its coil and badly crooked neck.
You don't know how you could ever have missed it.

You have to be careful not to touch them.
There is something called reflex biting,
which can happen even after the snake is dead.

* * *

I am driving and the destination is in sight. There is so much
traffic I am going 10 miles an hour. I look at the speedometer—it's
less. There is nothing I can do. There is no shortcut. I watch the
other people in their cars. I had been driving so fast and then it
just stopped. It never makes sense.

* * *

The heat of the day is melting the weeks of rain.
The air smells dank and rotten.
Everything is waterlogged.

I had done everything to be nice to him, with the thought that if he were happy, he would be a good father.
I made a huge mistake.

I had thought that the other would be a good stepfather, that we would have a family. I was wrong.

I try to turn it around.
I try to imagine that this is exactly what had to happen.

Imagine being so invisible that birds sit on your head,
like the statues at the Villa Borghese,
when it is so hot that only watermelon juice can save you.

Imagine the chunk of parmesan cheese being grated into small shavings, spread apart over the pasta, and then melting away.

Imagine being so raw that you go numb.

Imagine there is a boat that carries you into your sleep,
like the Egyptian boat that carries the dead.

Imagine the ghosts that walk through the Forum.

Imagine that everything is wrong, and you can do no right.

Imagine the angel comes to life from the painting,

it steps down and talks to you.

Imagine the large female bee, the queen bee, starving.

Imagine that you can't sleep—
it refuses to come to you
and you lie awake watching the light change.

Imagine Athena comes to life and storms the city.

Imagine you want to escape, you want to live the truth, you want
to leave your home town and jump on a ship that will go to sea
and take you to a new place.

Imagine Aphrodite awakens inside you, and you can't help
yourself.

Imagine that you have to learn a new language.

Imagine sitting under the sun until you overheat.

Imagine the drone of the bees high up in the tree, or in the bush
you pass, threatening to overtake you.

Imagine looking in the mirror and you are not sure what
happened.

Imagine that you go on deck and find that there is no one,
no captain, no crew members, no passengers.

Imagine eating spoon after spoon of thick white honey.

Imagine eating your soul.

Imagine that this is the new language—~~nothing~~.

* * *

And one day you look around and there is no land in sight.

In the Morning

1.

The slab of tire
lay on the shoulder
of the highway,
curled in resignation.

The patterns on the tires,
the tread, like the whorls
on the finger tip, inked
and pushed down
to leave a dark print
of a slammed brake.

The cars made them driving by.

2.

You slept on the side of the bed,
one of the sides, and I on the other,
backs against each other, vertebrae
interlocked like a jigsaw puzzle,
with the missing space
that became more than the image.

3.

Dear Mr. Brancusi,

At night your heads open their eyes.
They fly out over the ground
like forgotten shells

from an overturned bucket
near the ruins of a sand castle.

And in the morning,
the wings of moths
are swept up
from where you left
the candle.

For a While

She drove them back and forth all day, her children,
and it didn't take that much time unless there was traffic,
but the anticipation of the drives took up so much time
that the day was gone with the driving, consumed
by a giant snake that swallowed the cars on the freeway,
but where were they all going
if not toward a giant mouth like the entrance at the circus.

Dear Mr. Brancusi,

Dear Mr. Brancusi, oh Mr. Brancusi!

She threw herself on the blanket that covered the couch,
with drama like a woman in a garbage novel, like a woman
in a pointless situation, Madame Bovary, who cannot
escape her own paralysis, that showed in her dreams,
empty warehouses, with abandoned furniture, and maybe
one other person, with a scorched landscape, small fires
that erupted like sagebrush, colored red and orange
with a dark base, preparing to take flight to another
planet, but she was afraid because it required putting
on a spacesuit, that would be even more restricting
like a straitjacket, and she wondered if this was a sign
that something had to die, or that she was in fact dying.

Dear Mr. Brancusi,

Last year, at this time, I was preparing to go to Paris, not knowing
that I would meet you, not knowing that you would provide a safe
place for one moment, not realizing that the hotel room was going
to be like a room in an empty building. There was one window.
I remember the snow that came through when I opened It,
and left it open, and the courtyard below covered in snow,
small but big enough to sleep, under the white.

She stopped writing and looked around.
She was in a very American coffee shop,
sitting at the counter with bad coffee.

A Moment

My arms rest on a small round table
of dark blue and white tile squares;
the frame is made of black metal.

I reach to touch a glass salt and pepper shaker set.
The salt is almost empty. The pepper is full.

A wrought iron gate protects a wooden framed
glass paned door, both locked with pad locks.
I try to look inside, but can't see anything—
the glass is covered with a white curtain.

A fire extinguisher hides behind a potted palm,
but the sun slants through onto it, setting the red
on fire against the white wall, with a green leaf
that leans into the light to catch the ray
spreading its palm fingers that drift down,
relinquishing, a woman's hand that falls away.

And my shadow is there, too.
It is of my head as it leans
against the wall at an angle
as I look up.

It is the only thing that moves.

Earlier

The first lines woven into
the gray carpet looked
like scratches from all the bags
dragged to and from the gates,
to and from the airplanes,
to and from all the different
spots marked in red on the map.

The lines appeared to be
on top of a pattern of stripes
of alternating light and dark gray.

The chairs in the rows
with the arm rests,
the metal arms
that reach out to hold
each person that sat
and then left—
a momentary embrace
as the person sat back
with that slight gesture
of letting go
as the body falls back
into the body of the chair.

to find comfort
to find the tension spots
and try to address the—
to check the ticket or the time
or to look outside to see if the plane
has arrived, or moved, luggage loaded in.

Dear Mr. Brancusi,

Before all of that, at the security check, I was taken aside
and put in a space between two large panels, where I stood
barefoot with my arms up to be analyzed and scanned
by something I could not see. I was then sent to a woman
to hand check me. She asked if I had anything in my chest.
And she pointed with her rubber gloved finger at my heart.
I pulled down my shirt and showed her there was nothing.
She got very embarrassed and turned around to look for help.

No, don't do that, she said, as if I was taking my clothes off.
She wiped my hand with a cloth and put the cloth in a box.
What is that for, I asked. She said it was to see if I had touched
anything. I thought about it. I had touched many things.
She looked at me and told me I was done.
She moved her hands as if to say go on.

I turned around to gather my things
and put my shoes back on.
I went slowly. I had to think.

Mr. Brancusi, do you see what I am saying?

They detected something, but there was nothing.
I haven't touched anything, but I have.
If something was there, that they detected,
then what was it? What is it?
For a moment I thought the energy
of my chest, or movement of molecules,
had created a metallic resonance
that the machine picked up.

I imagined looking inside my chest
to see what rested in my ribs,
so white, like your sculptures,

and thought of you, and them,
and that I had rolled something
in all the breathing like the tide
until a smooth stone was created,
like the heads you sculpted
that lean against the shelves
near the exit of your atelier.

There is a party at someone else's house up the hill.
People are laughing outside.

The Two Balloons

The two white balloons hung above the vineyard with streamers
falling down from them, a giant jellyfish in the sky,
a Portuguese Man of War that swims above future wine
dripping poisons that will taste of the sea and mermaids.

The moon is low and heavy, resting on the dirt path
and the coyote dares me to walk into the dark canyon.

The woman cries and cries because she cannot get in the car
and drive one more time with five percent of the brakes left;
the mechanic had said that was the equivalent of five hundred
miles, but it wasn't the car or the brakes—it was the vacuum
that kept pulling at her and keeping her from taking a breath.

The deer had been eating the roses and the stems pushed long
and hard, becoming thin and stalky, to try to get away and find
a place to push the buds through and let them blossom.

And the balloons were over them now, because of the wind,
the streamers tangled in the chewed at branches,
with the two white heads rubbing against each other.

Inside

The room was quiet.

It was the insects
who sent the grinding vibrations inside.
The wall creaked and shifted to adjust
from holding the weight of the new roof.
The dog sighed after climbing onto the bed
with hesitant movements from old bones.
The fingers pushed on the black squares
that held each letter, making a gentle click
when they were touched.
But the room was quiet.
It was quiet.

Dear Mr. Brancusi,
I lean against you as I write.

She leaned against nothing
but an imaginary man.

A man who died alone.

I wrote this before,
but I will write it again—

I am sorry that you died alone.

The boy told the mother she was stupid.
You are an idiot. I am not hungry and I won't be,
when she tried to buy him something to take on
the plane that was flying from Los Angeles to New York.
You are wasting your money, he said. He sat down,
took a book out of his backpack and began to read.
She stood there watching him, then she walked away,

returning 15 minutes later with food to be wasted.

I don't want to die alone.
That is what she meant—
I don't want to live alone.

When the door closes, it pushes air across the hall,
into the other room, where a chime hangs near a window,

where the branch of sage that lay under the pillow
smelled like the day, and it begins to murmur and make soft
sounds that drown away the shadows falling from the unmade
bed—

Dear Mr. Brancusi,

Maybe you didn't die alone.
There is a picture where you are old and a young woman
sits in front of you. She is curved like a wilting flower,
as though melting in your presence, as though becoming herself
a receptacle for you.
A young Romanian couple took care of you as death waited
patiently in your studio, walking around, looking at your
sculptures. And you left everything to them, and your studio to
Paris.
Maybe you were happy and content, planning everything in a
painstaking way, similar to your obsession with reworking stone.

I will never know.

Easter 2011

The dog, so intent on killing the kittens
was not even distracted by bacon flavor
treats, soft chewy bones, in a foil packet
that sealed shut at the edges when pressed.

I am sure
Plato was right
when he said that love is a serious
mental disease.

From pictures it appears
to be shot into a person
with poisoned arrows
by a fat little naked boy.

As someone recovering
from the poison, I have
great compassion,
and I am jealous
that my blindness has worn off.

One Day

The wind that blows here blows over there, too.
As it moves on this continent it affects the other
continents, a swirling mass from a satellite's
perspective.

The grass has grown too high,
uncut; it has grown untended.

The car windows keep getting dirty and the car
itself is covered in dust that makes it look green.
It is a dark gray car, the color of empty ventricles.

* * *

The curve from the 101 North onto the 405 South
is a small oasis where the trees create caves
and the sound of desperate cars goes away
into the empty bottle, buried in the sand,
that holds a handwritten message in red ink
with speckles of gold.

* * *

Fresh baked bread with unsalted butter on a white plate.

Crumbs from the crust scatter.

A bird sits under the table.

* * *

Viewers go to see the sign everyday,
from below looking like a cardboard cutout
backed up by toothpicks.
They take pictures of themselves with it behind them,
oblivious to the underneath or anywhere outside
the viewfinder—cars askew at the curb blocking others
and the dogs trying to walk past the people,
past the path, past the bamboo grove,
between the dark movements of birds
that fly one way or another,
directions that make no sense,

and call or mimic a call,
the crystalline laugh of the coyote
breaking down into glass pieces
that cut somewhere behind, like the belt buckle
as the child ran as fast as she could,
to escape the hand that reached for her arm,
as she ran again, her back webbed with fear,
fear of the entrance into the grove,
small and dark, cool air coming out,
fear of the dare to go in and come out
on the other side, still alive,
as a deer lands startled by the dogs
where it landed, the doors marked on the map
of the plane's interior, and note them
before take off, into the other side of the path,
to leave the honeysuckle of radiant perfume,
its perfume that spikes in arches of a halo,
no color, maybe yellow, around the black Madonna's head,
painted to hold the shadow of all the people.

Forgiveness.
The music teacher who sat with her
saying that he knew what was happening,
he was her neighbor, he heard—
forgotten, in a niche in the church,
surrounded by burnt down candles.

* * *

Black tea with cream and sugar.

* * *

The hotel room was in Bagno Vignoni.
It was a converted stable. He lay in bed
while his wife went to the waters and painted.
She took pictures of him from the street
after she had thrown a pebble up to the window
and called for him to lean out, and, in the moment
of the click, knew that it was all wrong,
that she had framed it perfectly in the rectangle
of the tiny window of glass, composed,
but incorrect as it should have been her,
as she wanted it to be her, as she had wanted him
to photograph her, to want her—to think,

Jesus Christ, I am where the Etruscans went
to heal themselves, the Greeks, the Romans,
the pilgrims, the wounded warriors,
and I have this woman, this wife I would kill for,

a nice fairy tale, a myth about true love carved
on a cave wall signed with a bloody hand.
I want to remember this forever, this woman,
and the camera clicked as it was wrong,
and she looked, when she should have run
or screamed, but you promised, she would say
a year later, you said that you, and she heard it
and knew it wasn't what was being said;
she stayed, the person who was claiming
a true love, but it wasn't any less than a head
shoved against the wall and the hand reaching
to grab, so she laughed and made a joke,
more dangerous than a scream.
She held the camera and watched the scene
through it, then she stopped,
looked behind her at the old Italian couple
and she shrugged and they nodded.
She laughed and made jokes, Ah si, Romeo,
Romeo; she called to make them laugh
because what was the option—the truth,
that the waters had healed her
and she wasn't blind?

I don't understand

why it is this way,
now,
two years later—

       * * *

Four Cypress trees spear the sky

next to a billboard, braced
by wooden beams that lean
at a 45 degree angle,
an upside down guillotine
that cuts the sky into sections.

       * * *

Dear Mr. Brancusi,
the letter began,
I love you.
I am sorry that you died alone.
It continued,
I will live for you,
all your missed moments—

Rain

It rained this morning.
It's supposed to sprinkle throughout the day
and there is a ninety percent chance of rain
tomorrow, with one inch of rain expected.

They plot and study this, the weather people,
as they watch the clouds and winds turn around
the earth with changing temperatures and pressures.

It is a science experiment
I live in—
a finished cup of Turkish Coffee
that someone turns around
in their hand, looking for symbols
in the mud that foretell my future.

The Milk

The caul of boiled milk floats in the pan,
left over from last night, still waiting
to merge with dark coffee, black reflecting
ponds in the woods after the storm.

The coffee pot, old and stained,
un-screwed with the grinds
still packed in the cup,
some cold bubbled over coffee,
and the lower section calcified,
on its side, having been used.

Everything else has been cleaned
and put away.

I swirl the pot with left over milk
and watch the membrane slide,
attaching to the side, and then
letting go, debating whether or
not it might still be good
if I heated it up.

But it is so thick. It looks alive
now, coming out first before the child,
or on the child's head, now an animal's
head, with horns and yellow eyes
watching me from underneath—
a mirror, like the one at the gallery
that made the people on the other
side walking past look like ghosts.

I left it there, in the kitchen,
and walked the dogs where
the rained on Cedar smelled like

Holland and the gardens in Paris.

Dear Mr. Brancusi—

She wrote again. It had been a long time.

The smell of the air also reminded me of Rome
in the winter and I was wondering if you ever

worked there, and why you didn't, as your pieces
hold the beginning memories of the Cycladic figures.

The Kiss

1.
As the dog stepped across the room,
it made the sound of paper tearing,
pieces rubbing against each other
yet ripped apart, unwoven papyrus
shreds that fall away from the plant.

2.
The tree raises the rocks
from the ground
in concentric circles—
ripples of water
that radiate out
from the thrown pebble
on its last skip,
now going down
through the water
gravity to land
and dislodge dirt
sprayed in slow motion—

I follow the arc of one piece—

placed once
when it was first planted
a sapling
watered and watched
for new growth
to make sure it had rooted.

and the roots
are mountainous snakes
that lie still.

3.
I saw the cliff as I crossed the Mulholland Bridge over the 101.
There was a fissure, vertical, tilted at a slight angle, so the two
edges were slightly separate with a gentle shift, like the woman
against the wall, and yet together, like the sculpture you made,
The Kiss that has been turned into romance and, so, ruined.

4.
The man stooped, took a breath, and hoisted up the garbage
container, as he might have earlier a woman against the wall,
onto his right shoulder.

5.
On the radio, as I turn it on, is applause, the ocean sound
scrambled, and an announcement of the winner, a Mr. So and So,
baritonist from someplace. My mind wanders. I am not listening,
and then again,
his father played for the philharmonic, somewhere, and now I
am watching for the light to turn green when it seems he said the
mother was a laundress and his father referred to her as a fucking
whore, but that can't be, and I turn left, wondering what would
happen if it was.

6.
Mr. Brancusi,

I send you a kiss.

The Mirror

In the right side mirror of the truck
that I watch as I sit in traffic in the truck's shadow,
a rectangle is suspended in the sky, white
like the air right now, with too much sun
that bleaches out the blue and every other color.

A man is reflected in the mirror.
He is smoking. The cigarette is in his right hand—
it moves across the small rectangle
to his mouth and lingers
as the head tilts back to let the cloud come out and disappear,

as it leaves the reflecting pond
in the sky.

Incidental

I am going to write these words very slowly:
Nothing. Has. Changed.

I read them back, slowly. I have sat by myself in coffee shops
in New York with very little money,
enough for a coffee and a toasted corn muffin. I am sitting again
in a coffee shop, only now I am in Los Angeles,
and my son, who is larger than I am, sits to my left.

Listen, I am going to write this slowly too:
I am writing it in the coffee shop.

The feelings inside of me are the same. Nothing has changed.

All the men and other places and I don't know, all the I don't
knows, insignificant for memory, but still part of it—they have
made no difference. Something is wrong here because I know
that the only thing that doesn't change is change itself. I look up
and make eye contact with my son. He asks if I am crying. I tell
him no, I—I have something in my eye. I have been waking up
with my eyes full of all sorts of things.

      * * *

In an attempt to practice Viktor Frankl's Paradoxical Intention,
a layman's (mine) version of the technique,
and getting nowhere because I could not number all the anxieties
and fears. There seemed to be too many
and even boiling them down was not working. I found myself
responding to myself as my first therapist,
Dr. Gerry Greenwald, had one session. He'd said, "And then
what," to each thing that I said, until I said,

"I don't know, I guess I die." And then what? I don't know, I guess
I'm floating around in space.
And then what? Near the moon and the planets, I don't know.
And then what? I don't know. And then what? I can't remember
anymore how I responded because the end was not the end.
There was no end.
And that is where I ended in these thoughts. Ok, I'll be alone
forever floating in space. And then what,
I asked myself, because what else am I going to think of,
other than that I am old, ugly, alone, out of luck,
no money, the end; so what do I do based on that,
because killing myself is simply jumping the
gun.
I will die whether I want to or not, and these thoughts are
becoming pointless. And then what? I'll be dead. And then what?
I'll be floating around space, and how many times do I need to
say that
or think of that. Alone. Indefinitely. And then what? I guess I'll go
back and start over on earth
because the struggle and the emotions are better than the real
aloneness of nothing, of the nothing
of floating in outer space. And then I thought of reincarnation—
perhaps that's why people keep
coming back because the struggle alone is better than the reality
of the being alone in all of the nothingness.

      * * *

The entire walk takes about 45 minutes
It is circular, surrounded by mountains,
with a partial dirt path and some sidewalk.
The ocean is visible from two points.

The Fall

Dear Mr. Brancusi,

she began.

It is Fall here, and yet it is not.
It is 106 degrees in the Valley.
The sycamore's leaves are dry
and turn yellow ochre to match
the trunk, at the base of which
is an eye socket where a branch
once was, the beginning of a forked
trunk, dry and white, raised around
the edges, a healed scab, the thickened
skin of a scar.

Her fingernails were not perfect ovals.
She looked at them as she wrote,
small uneven faces,

Modigliani's eyeless women reclined
on the steering wheel.

She took a left onto the street
before the street she was supposed to take a left on
and found herself next to a convent.

She stopped the car and looked through the window.

It was peaceful—

it could have been in Europe
instead of the middle of Los Angeles;

it could have been anywhere but here.

She continued.

It had grown dark as I waited in the lights so bright they pulsated.
The room in the large building that housed shops, music,
and perfume that came from everywhere. They call it a mall.
It is like the labyrinth that housed the Minotaur.

I waited for help with my computer.

And when I walked to my car, it had grown dark.

I had missed the change.

While

The door was a fraud
and did not open;
it discreetly slid into the wall and hid.

Trickery.

Oh! Dear Mr. Brancusi,
if only you could be here
to see all of this.

The vernissage was to the left,
a large window straight ahead
avoided by a quick turn to the right.

If you were with me,
your world would have been—

She was interrupted.

The show was
avoided by a turn to the right,
or a lean against the wall of a window,
like a bird,
wings splayed open like fingers
reaching for the other side.

It would be simple to turn around
and follow the trail back to
where it started, and start over.
It would be simple, but it is difficult
and requires patience,
the acknowledgement of having gone the wrong way
when on the other side
of the glass, the destination appears to be

right there, in reaching distance,
touchable.
Susurrus;
it calls to you from the other side.

Only you would understand,
Mr. Brancusi.
It is like erasing the paper you spent hours on,

painting over the canvas,
grinding the stone back down to the stone.

The head leans to the side on the pillow
as though in reaction to a slap.

There is always a point where voices
no longer exist, all of them asleep
like the birds in the trees
when the sun has finally dropped.
Outside trucks pass each other
in abandoned streets,
lying flat and gray like the one the lover left.

If you were here with me now,
we would go for a walk.

Wheels jar the metal covers to the underground
entry ways to the tunnels and sewers of the city.
One clang calls to another,
like two Tibetan singing bowls,
the secret thoughts of the dreamers
that find each other.

I am going to go to sleep now.

The Moon

The moon is a reflective speck
on a black fish's gray scales.

The moon is a piece of silver
in curdled milk left outside
in a black bowl.

The moon is naked behind seven veils.

The moon is a fingernail clipping
blown across an asphalt road.

The moon is a piece of tooth
in a dark smile.

The moon is a scrap of paper
that did not burn in the fireplace.

The moon is a Brancusi head
lying on the shelf
in the darkened atelier
next to the Pompidou.

It snows outside
and some people sleep
but others walk
looking up at the sky
in disbelief.

The Cold

The water runs through the pipes,
one end of the house to another,
a long metal snake of the freeway traffic
in the setting sun, small sparks
of light from the scales
for moments reflect
the departure of the day.

The abandonment of light—
it leaves without saying goodbye.

And then

I cannot bear for it to get light—
the arms are Akhenaten's depiction
of the sun that reach out, reach in,
as I beg for it to stay
one moment longer.

I am not ready to begin,

and find that as it grows dark,
I feel a relief.

Thanksgiving

It was Thanksgiving and a football team
of grown men played in the dog park
that was low in a canyon below the mountain
and the sign with flashing lights around it.

She walked by all the people with her dogs
and looked at them, but they did not see her.

Dear Mr. Brancusi.

She began to write to him
but could not think of what to say
this time.

She walked by the dog park and watched the people.
The men yelled and jumped on each other.

The sky was getting darker.
There were a lot of cars parked near the houses
but there was no sound from the inside, no laughter.

This time, I am going to tell the truth.

Four trees were shedding yellow leaves,
bright against the charcoal sky.

She walked by other people walking their dogs
who looked in her direction as though they had heard something,
but could see nothing.

Dear Mr. Brancusi,

My children are in New York.

The moon is new.

This time there was no traffic—
the freeway drove like a miniature race track
with cars operated by handheld devices,
red, blue, and yellow with black stripes,
and the smell of electricity and oil.

She walked with her dogs
into the dark.

The Letters

I held three letters in my hand,
a spongy substance
that crumbled when I cut it.

She overheard—
You promised, the child said
and the mother had no answer.

She watched the light come on her phone
signifying that there was a message,
and she waited before she read it—

texted pictures of her children with the new sister,
feeding it from a bottle, posters for unwed
teenagers and American Apparel ads that leave
the viewer feeling nauseous.

My foot caught in the wood
and I heard the sound that should not
come from any part of my body;
the pain came in sharp after the sound
like thunder close after the lightening
and I lay there holding it.

Dear Mr. Brancusi,

I watched my toe change color
over the next three days.
Unlike your clean white sculptures,
I am blotched purple and red,
swollen and asymmetrical.

There are dragons, I had argued once
with my children grown skeptical

on the white and yellow checked floor
of the kitchen in the old house.
Look the word up in the dictionary.
It exists. Look at art from any culture
and there they are. Prove to me, then,
that they do not exist—
with drama, great drama,
j'accuse.

I wanted it more than them.

Dear Mr. Brancusi,

In the airport people gather at the gates.
Christmas music plays as alarms go off.
A steady high pitch stream is the undercurrent.
The people get into the planes,
and then there is nobody.
I sit, read, and wait for the plane.

When I close my eyes I see that I am flying
to Paris. I am in the hotel now, and I prepare
to walk to you. The Pompidou is a little
complicated from the Musée Rodin.

I see the entrance and I enter.
I walk clockwise and sit on
the cement bench and I look
into your studio and imagine.

When I open my eyes I am back in Los Angeles.

A man sits and works on his laptop.

A couple sits forehead to forehead
over a small table. I thought they were praying,
but when I got closer I saw they were looking
at something on a handheld device.

Another couple lies on the carpet,
near an electrical outlet, as their
computers charge. They lie as though
in the snow making snow angels.

The woman holds the coffee
and looks out the window.
She checks the time on her watch.

Today my blood has become heavy
and I need to lie down and sleep.

Reconciliation

On Sunday, I unrolled the canvases that I had taken off stretchers
to make room for when I was going to live with him, for when
he was moving into the house. It was three years ago that I rolled
them up, though it ended seven months ago with him. I did it, with
misgivings, as blindly as when I strung a chair crookedly, knowing
I would be punished for it and made to do it again. Unrolling the
canvases, paint stuck to the sides that it had pressed up against
for all this time, torn away, now raw and cracking,
was like peeling off a scab and seeing the scar that would stay
white forever, and the pain, and cringing. I cry as I write this.
My son helped me and I swore out loud and I told him never
to do something so self destructive for anyone. The end.

Dear Mr. Brancusi,

Outside the gardener is using the leaf blower and mowing
at the same time. I don't know if it is possible, but it sounds
that way. A fly is buzzing against the screen at the window.

I have seen a photo of Vera, Nabokov's wife, sitting at a
table near a window in Paris, and I am trying to pretend
that I am in an apartment like that, writing to you.

The woman tried to write
as her son paced outside
making battle noises,
as he had been doing
for 15 years, reenactments
of scenes from famous wars.
She bought him the collection
of writings of Winston Churchill
for Christmas one year ago.

The Magic Mountain

The sky makes a right angle above me;
my back leans into a surface that will not give.

One of the plants in the front yard is dying. I
 don't know why.
I don't know its name.

I lie in a blanket in a chair, outside,
like the main character
in *The Magic Mountain.*

I look at the trees against the sky,
the shape the sky makes between them,
inverted bluish trees,

a hand with sharpened nails,
like talons, that point down,
as if to indicate that it is here,
this spot on the map.

The Counter

The counter makes a wide U shape; the top is formica
in the pattern of light wood burnished red. The waitresses
wear gray dresses down to their knees and stockings
under their socks, with aprons from another time.

Their hair is pulled back, topped with small white caps
with the name of the place embroidered on it. The cooks
wear hair nets and shower caps.

Black and white photographs of people from another time
standing in groups hang on the walls. One wall is mirrored
and the booths have red naugahyde seats with floating tables.

The carpet is dark green with a floral and leaf pattern.
The coffee is bitter and even with cream the taste stays.

There is a small placard on the counter, held in a plastic frame,
that shows a picture of chunks of pineapple in a pineapple
that has been halved and hollowed, emptied and turned into
a bowl, that says Pineapple Fruit Pie. It could be chunks of butter.

The ceiling is gridded into squares with metal—
within each square is a square of a some kind of material,
white with small black holes the reverse of the night sky.

The waitress says, "Any more coffee sweetie," and I say, "Yes,"
because she seems to be trying to be nice and do her job.

Dear Mr. Brancusi,
I hate this place. It makes me sick, the coffee tastes like bile and I
can't digest it. Everyone walks in with someone; families sit down
and smile at one another while the mother asks the child

what it wants. Do you want scrambled eggs?
Do you want a pancake? Do you want milk or orange juice?
How about a pancake and a side of scrambled eggs?
And the child nods, magnetized by something behind the counter,
the bustling cooks and waitresses—I hate that word, bustling; it
makes me think of Norman Rockwell.

And what I would give to lean my head on your shoulder and
watch you draw, work on the disintegration of the human form,
the human head into its essence,
into a beautiful plaster egg shape, oblivious to any of this,
and maybe you would look up
and smile at me and I would think of stringing a washing line
across the yard to hang clothes to dry.
I will fill the yard with lines and hang white sheets
and watch the wind push them against me to find the form of
a standing figure, of the figures in Pompeii, that lie covered in
volcanic ash, dreaming, arms curved, legs bent,
the egg shaped head in the sun reflected white,
repose of stillness, the human form.

The Soul

I.

I was trying to get at something,
being cold and holding my body
in with tensed muscles,
as if it would make me warmer,
as if being warm I would have found
what I was looking for.

I remember the river, La Seine,
as the sun was not quite there,
leaving to go somewhere else,
the air turned gold, the river lit
up like an emerging whale
covered in gold leaf.

And that night in the maze as it snowed—
it was dark, but the moon must have been full,
reflecting off the ground, lighting the path,
but still dark enough that I was frightened.
No, wary of what might happen,
and my shoulders hurt from all of it.

I kept looking for a sign.

II.

BA Self Storage was to the left as I drove South on the 101,
I think it is somewhere near the Vermont exit.
I wrote it down. There was so much traffic, I could do that—
find a pen, my book that I constructed from left over paper
piled on a plastic bin near the printer.

The sign was big on the billboard and ugly like all the others
trailing in the wake of the freeway, with me pretending
I am in Paris, where maybe the billboards are less offensive.
I remember a Garnier one on a bus and a small poster
where the moon had a face with a locomotive in the eye.

III

The Greek sculptures that I love so much remind me of you.

They are white and some almost abstract, modernized,
like the poet as Orpheus with his blank stare, stylized
into an early Picasso. I feel as though I am seeing the human
in its essence without the groceries and the laundry.

When I read the plaque I see that I am wrong—they were painted,
brightly. I know from art history they were gaudily painted, gaudily,
a word that brings awkward color and abandon, and right now
I wonder if maybe that is a good thing because the concentration
and discipline needed to continually strip away the unnecessary
to get to the essence can, on occasion, leave out the life.

I try to imagine Praxiteles' Aphrodite painted gaudily
and with wild abandon, I try to embrace it, and enjoy it.

I try to embrace the ceaseless driving I do everyday,
a hamster on a treadmill that does not swoop over,
like the owl on the way to the rat chattering behind
the watering can, in circles that go nowhere but back
and onto the circle, the endless cycle of the diameter.

With wild abandon I enter my car, my lips painted red
like the dyed hair of an old Parisian whore that I have made

up in my mind, or the red of the witch that everybody points to
who lives at the end of the cul-de-sac and lies in the pines praying
to all the gods.

You were there when I entered the atelier
with nowhere else to go.
The fat bird still eating the crumbs of the crepe suzette
my children had dropped, and deliberately fed,
and the leftover wine
I drank to try to soften the feeling in the air
that nothing was left but to follow a map
to go from one destination to another, but not you,
never you, until someone told me about you.
I ran away like you did when you were young.

I sat and looked into your life through glass panels for free.
I imagined that I could step in and you would be there
and I could pick up a stone and you would show me how to grind
it smooth until nothing was left but powder that would blow across
the square when we opened the doors.

I try to recreate how it happened

I was In Paris, it was snowing, and had not done so in years.
We arrived at night and after drinking Angelina's chocolate,
walked to the Louvre. It was snowing. My feet were wet
and cold. There were hardly any footprints in the maze.

I felt lost.

After two days in the city where I had dreamt I would live,
I hated it and wanted to go home, but had forgotten where
that was; I had been searching for it in the maze for years.

We went to your atelier and I sat on the bench
outside the glass windows, erected to keep
the animals out and the art safe,
and I wept when no one was looking,
when they had turned the corner.

I am talking to you.

I write to you.

I call to you.

You do not answer because this needs to be one sided.

I read about you and saw we share certain things.

I thought you might love me as I love you,
when I don't love you. I am not even in love
with your art and at first had you confused
with Noguchi. But I like the wearing down of the form
like the ocean to a piece of glass or rock,
the water melting and pushing continents apart.

It was just that I thought perhaps a dead person could love me.

Incessant pain crawls up my vertebrae, a crested snake,
and if I could escape I would, slough it off into blue
water where yours would be white forms lined neatly
on the shelves, my head at an angle, features simplified.

I do not love you.

I do not even know you.

I only love the stillness of your impeccable space
in the street stained by the Revolution.

And if there is nothing, as discovered blocks away
in a café after you were dead by French intellectuals,
and if there is nothing after the car crashed, overturned,
then I am only here, or there, writing to you, nonexistence
folded over into the air of the croissant and dipped
into the sugar chocolate to sweep away the night before
of red wine from a carafe that is refilled until there is light,

but the wall open to the garden that walks into the mountain
that touches the goddess who holds the sky and swallows
the sun and the moon, birthed by the mountain,
of the mountain, and into the mountain.

Before

I had wanted to sit
and feel safe.
I had wanted the ceaseless
traveling to stop.

I had wanted someone
so that I did not have to be alone.

This is one sided.

I am writing to you
and you are dead.

I am writing to a person
who filled these empty rooms.

I am writing a person
who ground shapes down to the end.

I am writing to someone.

One year ago,
you thought you would try to do something in the hotel
that night when you cried in the bathtub and could not sleep,
you thought you would try to write it.

I am writing to a space held in a glass walled room
a snow globe with the white settled on the floor.

I am writing to a possibility.

Then

The dusty window goes opaque
when the sun hits it.

I hated the hotel,
my feet were wet and cold from the snow.
Your atelier was a stop in a breath,
an intake before what would come after.

I couldn't see anything properly.
It was so clean with tools set in place.

I looked through the glass
as I had looked into warm windows
at night from the street.

Some of the pieces rested on the shelves.
They were so smooth and clean and white.

Everything about me felt dark like the night when
I walked through the maze in the snow,
the carousel in the distance with spots of white
paint that the impressionist's brush had left
as it rolled off the table.

A Stranger

I tried to take her sickness,
and his before hers.
I drank from every glass
of water I brought to them
after the pill was swallowed
and the head turned to the side,
the hand on the arm extended
with the glass for me to take
and leave.

I drank it.

I watched how the fever
calmed them into focus
of sleep and submission
into bird feathers wrapped
in cotton.

I followed the visitor into the street
and asked when the last time was
that she had let go
that she had submitted to something
with complete
commitment to abandon
abandon the wrong word
the word is not the word

but the fall.

I thought if I could get that sick
I would find you.

If everything went away
I could find you.

You would magically appear
to take care of me and love me
a romantic notion
the kind I hate when I hear or read it.
I am embarrassed to be writing it.
You would not.
You would not even acknowledge a child you had
with one of your women.

And.
I do not want to be anymore
one of your women
as when, at 11, I no longer wanted to be a nun
married to Jesus
and at 11 I lay in bed wondering who it would be then.
I tried many but none of them worked
naked in the oval hidden by the oleanders.

At 11.

I walked in undiagnosed depression
abuse in my elbows
and broken shoulder blade
that tried to push as an infant.

I will sand the wooden block until it is smooth.
I will walk alone in Paris
when it is ugly and cold.
I will walk and sit and look.
I will put my hand on the dark wood
and reach for the cup
of tea
or coffee
or wine

or nothing.

I will reach out with my eyes
lintel ears.

I will listen to the numb air.

A stranger.

Inside the Glass

Inside is warm.
The guard gives us the brochure and waves us in.
It is free. He wants to know what we are waiting for.
There isn't a lot of color.
It could be an Egyptian tomb, cracked open,
with the sun having bleached everything in sight,
but the stories are still carved out
on the walls and heads on shelves.

Your hand might have lifted that saw
and placed it on the nail.

You slept up the steps in the loft.

I write to you.

I am trying to bring you back to life.

The cold outside,
the melted snow in the streets,
leaning against the curb,

and I talk to you.

My children are sitting on the other side.

For a moment it is just me,
pressed up against the glass.

In Between

In between the walls were images.

I looked you up and read about you
when I got back to the hotel.

The images played against
the white walls.

I thought if I could connect to you
that I would be able to bring order into my life,
that it would be clean and white,
that it would make sense.

Images of dinner parties in your atelier.

I thought if I devoted myself to you
that my life would have purpose.

Images of you sitting and working,
holding the plaster in your hands.

I write with a purple Stabilo pen.

Jeanne d'Arc

Jeanne d'Arc's cape curls behind in the wind,
up and over with the tip that comes down
on the back of the horse, creating a circle
of space that I bend down and step through.

There is no quiet anymore—
the clock ticks.

My blood pushes through my ear.
I feel it—
yellow lights inside for night travel
barricades up to prevent the earth
from caving in
the lintel that holds the arch
my head the keystone of the arch of my body
my head of a weight—

I sand the wooden block
to try to erase the cut marks.

The heaviness of the air has a sound.

I heard it in your atelier.

You can't help me anymore.

I had a nightmare
two nights ago.

I can only strive now
to create as you did.

The Last Letter

The sidewalk had spots on it.
Most were circular, crushed spheres,
and in between were shiny spots
mixed in with the cement.
The sky reflected an altered
sky beneath my feet.

The heat dries the clothes
that hang from the white
line stretched between
the house and the tree.

The sheet sails up
and I walk through
to the other side

where it is hot in mid-winter
and a wind blows in crisscrosses,
making cat paws in the clouds,
and I am ill at ease

with nothing to hold on to.

You are gone,

but this moment.

This.

Melora **Walters** is a graduate of Pratt Institute.

She best known for her film and television career, appearing in iconic movies; *Boogie Nights, Magnolia, Cold Mountain* and *Dead Poet's Society* (amongst many others).

Her poems have been published by Finishing Line Press, Writ Large Press, Serpentine Press, DRYLAND Lit, and Levure Littéraire.

She has exhibited her art in New York, Los Angeles at Jan Baum Gallery, Merry Karnowsky Gallery-LA, Self Help Graphics, LAUNCH LA, and internationally at the Merry Karnowsky Gallery, Berlin.

Melora has two children, Tom and Joanna.

www.ingramcontent.com/pod-product-compliance
Lightning Source LLC
Chambersburg PA
CBHW021200090426
42740CB00008B/1171